S0-BFD-822

State Your Case

Evaluating Arguments About

Technology

Simon Rose

CRABTREE
PUBLISHING COMPANY
WWW.CRABTREEBOOKS.COM

State Your Case

Author: Simon Rose

Series research and development: Reagan Miller

Editors: Sarah Eason, Claudia Martin,
Jennifer Sanderson, and Janine Deschenes

Proofreaders: Tracey Kelly, Wendy Scavuzzo

Indexer: Tracey Kelly

Editorial director: Kathy Middleton

Design: Paul Myerscough

Cover design: Katherine Berti

Photo research: Claudia Martin

**Production coordinator and
Prepress technician:** Katherine Berti

Print coordinator: Katherine Berti

Produced for Crabtree Publishing Company
by Calcium Creative Ltd

Photo Credits:
t=Top, c=Center, b=Bottom, l=Left, r=Right.

Inside: Shutterstock: 06photo: p.24; A Aleksandravicius: p.12r;
Anatoliy Cherkas: p.7; Andrei Kholmov: p.5; Andrey Popov: p.30;
Antonio Guillem: p.36; BBernard: p.6; Beketoff: p.32; Belushi: p.18;
Billion Photos: p.13l; Bluskystudio: p.20; DiversityStudio: p.15;
Dmitriy Kalinovsky: p.27; Dragon Images: p.9; Drop of Light: p.35;
Ioan Florin Cnejevici: p.14; leungchopan: p.19; metamorworks: pp.16,
28; miya227: p.17; Monkey Business Images: pp.3, 8, 10, 11; muph:
p.26; Rawpixel.com: p.43; Samuel Borges Photography: p.38; Sasin
Tipchal: p.22; Scharfsinn: p.31; Sebastien Durand: p.29; sirtravelalot:
p.25; SpeedKingz: p.41; Tinnapong: p.37; Tyler Olson: p.42; vinnstock:
p.40; Volodymyr Baleha: p.33; vovan: p.13r; wavebreakmedia: p.39;
Wayhome Studio: p.4; Yakobchuk Viacheslav: pp.1, 21; Yalana: p.12l;
Zapp2Photo: pp.23, 34.

Cover: All images from Shutterstock

WITHDRAWN

Library and Archives Canada Cataloguing in Publication

Rose, Simon, 1961-, author
    Evaluating arguments about technology / Simon Rose.

(State your case)
Includes bibliographical references and index.
Issued in print and electronic formats.
ISBN 978-0-7787-5079-6 (hardcover).--
ISBN 978-0-7787-5104-5 (softcover).--
ISBN 978-1-4271-2164-6 (HTML)

    1. Technology--Juvenile literature. 2. Technology--Moral and
ethical aspects--Juvenile literature. 3. Critical thinking--
Juvenile literature. 4. Thought and thinking--Juvenile literature.
5. Reasoning—Juvenile literature. 6. Persuasion (Rhetoric)--
Juvenile literature. I. Title.

BJ59.R67 2018   j174'.96   C2018-903033-X
                                             C2018-903034-8

Library of Congress Cataloging-in-Publication Data

Names: Rose, Simon, 1961- author.
Title: Evaluating arguments about technology / Simon Rose.
Description: New York, New York : Crabtree Publishing Company,
  [2019] | Series: State your case |
  Includes bibliographical references and index.
Identifiers: LCCN 2018030280 (print) | LCCN 2018032292 (ebook) |
  ISBN 9781427121646 (Electronic) |
  ISBN 9780778750796 (hardcover) |
  ISBN 9780778751045 (pbk.)
Subjects: LCSH: Technology and civilization--Juvenile literature. |
  Technological innovations--Social aspects--Juvenile literature. |
  Technological innovations--Economic aspects--Juvenile literature.
Classification: LCC CB478 (ebook) | LCC CB478 .R63 2019 (print) |
  DDC 303.48/3--dc23
LC record available at https://lccn.loc.gov/2018030280

Crabtree Publishing Company
www.crabtreebooks.com   1-800-387-7650

Printed in the U.S.A./092018/CG20180810

Copyright © **2019 CRABTREE PUBLISHING COMPANY**. All rights reserved. No part of this publication may be reproduced, stored in a retrieval
system, or be transmitted in any form or by any means, electronic, mechanical, photocopying, recording, or otherwise, without the prior written
permission of Crabtree Publishing Company. In Canada: We acknowledge the financial support of the Government of Canada through the
Canada Book Fund for our publishing activities.

Published in Canada
Crabtree Publishing
616 Welland Ave.
St. Catharines, Ontario
L2M 5V6

Published in the United States
Crabtree Publishing
PMB 59051
350 Fifth Avenue, 59th Floor
New York, New York 10118

Published in the United Kingdom
Crabtree Publishing
Maritime House
Basin Road North, Hove
BN41 1WR

Published in Australia
Crabtree Publishing
3 Charles Street
Coburg North
VIC, 3058

CONTENTS

Most of us use technology every day. Think about a smartphone. We use it to communicate with each other. But we also watch television on it, play games on it, and even use it to order food! Think of all the technology we use at home, too, from televisions and microwave ovens to hairdryers and computers. Technology has changed the way that we live.

Everything Has Changed

Thirty years ago, there were no websites, very few people had cell phones, and most people did not own their own computer. That has all changed! Today, we talk to our friends and family through Facebook and Snapchat, we upload photographs to Instagram, send text messages and images on our phones, post updates to Twitter, and create videos for YouTube. Sometimes, we even "speak" in a different language when we communicate using text abbreviations, symbols, and emojis.

Computer technology is changing all the time. At home, voice commands might soon be used to turn on lights, dishwashers, televisions, and more. Already, there are refrigerators that can reorder food when their shelves start to empty. New apps are invented all the time, **artificial intelligence (AI)** is making smartphones even smarter, and video games are becoming more realistic. **Virtual reality (VR)** is already here, allowing us to experience digital worlds as if we are physically there.

Could you live without your smartphone? These devices can be used for more than keeping in touch with friends. They can make daily tasks, such as shopping, very convenient.

Robots are used in most car factories today. In the future, they are likely to be used in many other industries.

Tech Saving Lives

Technology has also changed science and medicine. Medical technology can scan the body for illnesses, which helps save people's lives. **3-D printers** can create artificial limbs for people who have **disabilities**. Robotic machines can test samples or measure out tiny quantities of medicine. Computer programs can map out how **epidemics** of diseases spread, so they can be prevented.

Looking into the Future

In the next few decades, we are likely to ride in **driverless cars**. There will also be more **drones** in the skies above our towns and cities. Police forces, security and delivery companies, moviemakers, photographers, and even farmers already use these for security scanning, for filming or taking pictures, and for carrying and delivering products.

In the future, computers and robots are likely to do more jobs in offices, restaurants, **factories**, and even schools. This is called **automation**. Automation will make some businesses more efficient, but it will also mean that the people who once did those jobs may have to find new jobs.

Teens and Technology

In the coming years, digital technology will become more ingrained in our day-to-day activities. Soon, we will rely on new technology to travel around, whether that is in driverless cars and buses or in oversized taxi drones. We will need to know how to use many different types of technology in our jobs. The ways we learn, communicate, and have fun may also change with updated technology. Learning about and being comfortable with technology will help us get ready for the high-tech future.

Technology: A Hot Topic

We know that technology will change our future and that there will be more technology than ever. But could more technology be harmful? There is concern that with the easiness of access to information online, children may access content that is not appropriate for them. **Social media** has allowed us to connect with each other in ways that were not possible before. But there are worries that it means we are spending less time with our family and friends and more time on our tablets and phones. Have we all become too dependent on technology?

Arguing About Technology

Scroll through your Facebook feed or flip on your local news network, and you will probably find people arguing about issues surrounding technology. You need to be able to **evaluate**, or carefully consider, the arguments you hear to decide which ones are **credible**—and which are not. That way, you can start to form your own opinions about technology and how it affects you.

In this book, we'll take a look at the arguments for and against technology. We'll look at the features of an argument, what makes a strong argument, and how to decide if you agree with it or not. Let's start by taking a look at the arguments about social media and personal relationships on the opposite page.

Playing video games with friends can allow us to connect with each other and have fun with technology. Can the same be said of social media, though?

Do You Agree?

"Does social media have a positive or negative effect on personal relationships?"

SOCIAL MEDIA HAS A POSITIVE EFFECT ON RELATIONSHIPS.

Social media allows people to connect with friends and family. People can reconnect with friends they have not seen for a long time, and stay in touch with family members who live in different places. Social media also allows people to talk to others with similar interests all around the world.

Technology performs a vital role in modern social relationships. In 2017, a poll by the charity Action for Children found that nearly half of 11- to 16-year-olds found it easier to be themselves online than face to face. Three out of five of the teens said that they would be lonely if they could not talk to their friends using technology.

SOCIAL MEDIA HAS A NEGATIVE EFFECT ON RELATIONSHIPS.

Social media sites mean that people spend less time together in person. Although people connect with others on social media, it also means that they are spending too much time alone. A poll taken in 2017 states that 6 out of 10 12- to-17-year-olds said that they were lonely. One in 20 children claimed that they never spent time with their friends outside of school.

Children who don't spend face-to-face time with their peers may have trouble developing social skills. Less face-to-face communication could mean that they do not notice facial expressions that can help them understand what the other person means. More than 40 percent of the attention we give to others in a conversation is related to their eyes. According to Dr. Catherine Steiner-Adair, communicating by text or through the Internet makes "body language, facial expression, and even the smallest kinds of vocal reactions [...] invisible."

After reading the arguments about whether social media has a positive or negative effect on personal relationships, decide which side you agree with. How did you make your choice? Did you rely on personal experience? Does the way the arguments are presented influence your decision?

CHAPTER 2

WHAT MAKES AN ARGUMENT?

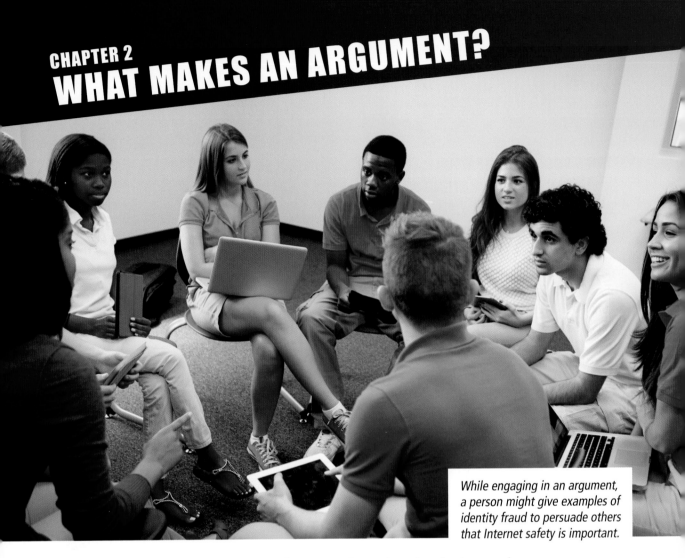

While engaging in an argument, a person might give examples of identity fraud to persuade others that Internet safety is important.

An argument is a reason or set of reasons based on **logic**. Its goal is to show that a person's belief or position on an issue is **valid**. An argument can be used to try to change another person's point of view or to persuade them to accept a new point of view. Arguments can also be used to draw support or promote action for a cause.

Why Argue?

You read, hear, and see arguments every day. For example, you might see two **politicians** on television arguing about rules for Internet safety. Each person states their ideas, gives their reasons, and, if the argument is strong, supports their reasons with **evidence** to try to persuade voters that their ideas are best.

Arguments can be used in different ways. Sometimes an argument can help people learn about an issue. It might explain one or both sides of an issue so people can make an informed decision about what they believe. For example, an argument that helps people learn about Internet safety might outline the risks of posting personal information online. Other arguments are used to gather support for a cause, such as the importance of recycling electronics. These are persuasive arguments. These arguments are also used to influence people to agree with certain beliefs. They are supposed to influence the way you think about something or change your mind about an issue. An argument about the benefits of smartphones might try to convince people that a smartphone is the best place to write down thoughts, because journals are often lost and smartphones are easily accessible.

Other arguments are designed to solve problems and make decisions. For example, members of a community might present arguments about which location is the best place to build a new school. Looking at both sides of an argument helps people decide how they should act on an issue.

Arguments are not always serious. Sometimes people present arguments just to learn about and discuss opposing ideas.

Prove Your Point

An argument is made up of a number of **claims**, or statements about why a viewpoint is correct. Claims need to be proven with evidence such as facts, **statistics**, and quotes from experts. Without evidence, there is no way to prove that your claims are true. When you are evaluating an argument, it is up to you to decide whether the person making the argument has supported their claims with evidence.

A person arguing for the benefits of electronic devices might say that they keep us more organized by giving daily reminders about appointments or events.

Building an Argument

A strong argument needs to be built carefully. Look for all of the following features, or parts, in a strong argument:

Core Argument

The **core argument** is your position, or where you stand, on the topic or issue. It states what you believe to be true and is the main point that you will try to prove in your argument. Arguments state the core argument in their introduction. An example of a core argument is:

> *Technology supports learning at school.*

> *Today, many students are taught how to **code** computer games. This encourages both logical and creative thinking.*

Claims

Your claims are the statements that support your core argument. An example of a claim is:

> *Using laptops and other devices in the classroom helps students build their reading and writing skills.*

Reasons

Reasons are details that support your claim. They explain why you have made that specific claim. An example of a reason is:

> *Laptops and other devices give students the creative tools they need to create and publish stories. They can use computer programs to connect words with images, and use spelling and story-building programs to support their writing.*

Evidence

A good argument supports its reasons with evidence. It might be a quotation from an interview with someone who is considered to be an expert on the topic. It might be statistics from a study of people affected by an issue, or facts about the topic. Without evidence, an argument cannot be proven to be true.

Not everything you read is credible, so you need to assess if the evidence is valid. You can do this by asking questions such as:
- Who is the author of the **source** of the information? Are they knowledgeable in the subject?
- Where did the information come from? Is it a respected organization?
- When was the source written? If it was several years ago, the information might be out of date.
- Do other sources have similar information? If not, you may need to evaluate whether the source is credible.

This is an example of credible evidence. It comes from a respected organization and someone who is knowledgeable in the subject.

Dr. Chrystalla Mouza, Professor of Instructional Technology at the School of Education at the University of Delaware, learned that elementary school students with access to laptops were able to create electronic storybooks and publish reports in language arts classrooms.

Counterclaims

To make an argument even stronger, a person needs to take note of the possible **counterclaims** against their argument. Counterclaims are claims that support the opposite viewpoint to the argument. After making claims and giving reasons and evidence, a person making an argument should write down the strongest counterclaim against their argument. They should then respond to the counterclaim, using evidence, to prove why their argument is stronger. This is an example of a counterclaim:

Some people argue that technology in the classroom is a distraction rather than a help. A report by the Organisation for Economic Co-operation and Development (OECD) in 2015 found that when not implemented correctly by teachers, technology could be a distraction. But as Dr. Chrystalla Mouza explained, students who used laptops in school were able to create stories and then publish them. When teachers are able to implement technology the right way, it is very useful in the classroom.

Conclusion

Your conclusion should restate your main argument and reasons. An example of a conclusion is:

Due to the benefits it has in helping students build their reading and writing skills, it is clear that technology supports learning at school.

Technology in schools can teach students the skills they will need in the workplace, from design techniques to operating 3-D printers.

Evaluating an Argument

You can evaluate an argument by looking at its features. Examine the argument below about e-books. Does the argument include all of the features it needs to be a strong argument? When you have finished reading, decide if you think this argument is strong.

CORE ARGUMENT

E-books are a better option than printed books and should replace them because they help struggling readers learn to read, and they are better for the environment.

CLAIM

E-books have technology that supports people who are learning to read.

REASON

Some e-books have a read-aloud option. This helps beginner readers learn new words and hear how they should be pronounced, or spoken. Some e-books also allow the reader to click on an unfamiliar word to learn its meaning. E-books can also be adapted to the needs of the reader. For example, you can adjust the font size or magnify the text to make it easier for people who struggle to read small type.

EVIDENCE

A 2015 study in the United Kingdom (UK) showed that being able to read e-books improved reading skills. After being given e-books, the number of boys who found reading difficult fell from 28 percent to 16 percent.

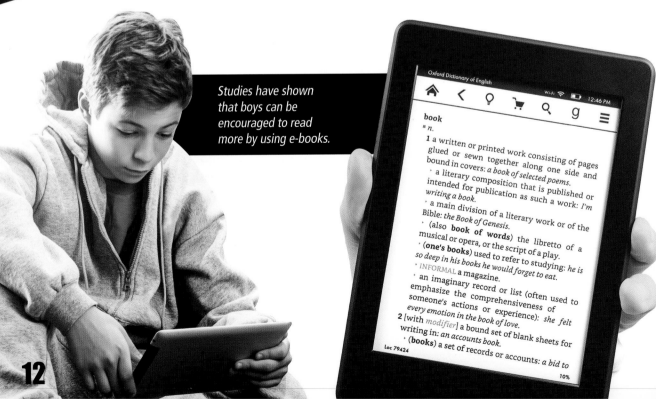

Studies have shown that boys can be encouraged to read more by using e-books.

One argument in favor of e-books is that they help preserve the environment.

CLAIM

E-books should replace printed books because they are better for the environment.

REASON

E-books are not printed on paper, so they do not require trees to be cut down to make them.

EVIDENCE

In the United States, around 2 billion books are made each year. To manufacture the paper for these books, 32 million trees are needed. One tree produces enough paper for approximately 62.5 books. This means that, if 200 million e-books are sold and downloaded, 3,200,000 trees will be saved.

COUNTERCLAIM

Some people argue that e-books should not replace printed books because reading books on devices opens up the opportunity to be distracted with other activities, such as games. Naomi Baron, Professor of Linguistics at American University, surveyed more than 300 university students in the U.S., Japan, Germany, and Slovakia regarding how they preferred to read. She found that 92 percent concentrated best when using printed books. However, evidence shows that reading skills can be improved by using the tools only available on e-books. Therefore, the effect e-books have on learning is more positive than negative.

CONCLUSION

Due to the benefits reading e-books has on learning and the environment, they should replace paper books. E-books will encourage more people to read, improve **literacy** around the world, reduce waste, and also help protect the planet for future generations.

Making a Great Argument

Core arguments, claims, reasons, evidence, counterclaims, and conclusions are the important parts of an argument. But there are also other elements that make a great argument.

Who Is Your Audience?

Knowing who your **audience** is will help you target your argument. This means that you can use language and make points that will connect with the people you are trying to convince. You can base your argument on details about your audience, such as their age, **gender**, or background.

People of different ages have different perspectives on issues. A teenager who has grown up with technology has a different view on social media than an older person. A person's lifestyle, including their job and where they live, also influences how they feel about certain issues. For example, a person working in car manufacturing might be worried about his or her job being taken over by a robot. A robot engineer might feel differently. When you make an argument, it is important to keep the perspective of your audience in mind and make sure that your claims and evidence will relate to them.

Introductions Count

Your introduction should get the reader interested in the topic and clearly introduce your main argument. An introduction should include a statement that interests the reader. For example, an argument in favor of e-books might state: "Did you know that 266 million e-books were sold in the United States in 2017?" Follow an interesting introductory statement with the core argument.

An argument in favor of e-books that is directed at an audience concerned about green issues might try to persuade them that e-books are Earth-friendly because they can replace large libraries that require a lot of electricity for lighting.

Clincher Conclusions

The conclusion is as important as your introduction. After restating your core argument and claims, your conclusion should end with a **clincher**. This is a statement that will strengthen your argument by capturing the reader's attention right at the end, so that they are more likely to consider all your points and agree with you.

For the e-book argument, your clincher could be:

> It is very clear that e-books are an excellent way to improve literacy and protect Earth for future generations.

A clincher can also be a quote or question that makes the reader think. For example:

> Shouldn't we all be interested in encouraging literacy and saving the planet for future generations?

Choose Your Words

The words you use and how you use them help you persuade people to see your point of view. Words can appeal to someone's emotions and strengthen the evidence that you present. For example, referring to sources of facts and statistics will back up your claims. Mentioning **qualified** experts and adding quotes from them can also make people more likely to believe you. Words can appeal to people's emotions by emphasizing or stressing things they care about. In the e-book argument, words might emphasize the damage to forests and wildlife caused by the production of paper to make books.

A great conclusion to an argument in favor of smartphones could be a question such as: "News can now be accessed anywhere with a smartphone. Isn't that a great thing?"

Powerful Words

How effective an argument is often depends on the types of words used. **Rhetoric** is the art of using language effectively when writing or speaking. Rhetoric is usually used in persuasive speaking or writing by appealing to a reader's or listener's emotions.

Persuasive Trio

There are three types of rhetoric: logos, pathos, and ethos.

Logos: Logos uses logic and reason to prove a point. Logos is a Greek word from which we get the word "logic." Writing with logos often requires the use of facts and statistics. A logical argument backed up with solid facts will help others consider your position, even if they do not agree with it. Here is an example of logos:

> *The statistics clearly show that over the last ten years, this technology has sold more than every one of its competitors.*

Pathos: Pathos uses emotion in the argument. Personal stories and connections are used to try to persuade others. For example, the story of a child or family that has suffered during a war might be more persuasive than the bigger picture of the war and the total number of people affected. Emotion should be used only to support your claim. It should not be used to confuse or frighten people in order to win an argument. Here is an example of pathos:

> *A parent's piece of mind is priceless. Our cell phone app will let you always know the location of your child, so that you know she is safe.*

Ethos: Ethos is the way that the person can establish that they can be trusted. The tone and style of their writing or speaking shows the person's qualifications and knowledge about an issue. Ethos often uses reliable sources, tells the audience about the person's expertise, and is respectful of the opposing view. All of these things can establish trust. Here is an example of ethos:

> *As a technician who has worked for ten years on the development of driverless vehicles, I am fully qualified to tell you that this car will deliver the best results.*

Would the above technician's quote persuade you to travel in a driverless car?

Pathos can be a powerful tool in an argument. It hooks into a person's strong emotions, such as their concern for their child.

LOOKING AT LANGUAGE

Read the following statement. Can you identify the rhetoric the author has used? What words or phrases make you think so?

Research over the last 20 years has consistently proved that this medical technology provides the most effective treatment for the condition. Our expertise in medical devices is proven by our 50 years in the **industry**, our highly qualified technicians, and our satisfied clients. We all want our families to be safe and well. This technology will ensure that your loved ones will be receiving the very best treatment available.

Where Do You Stand?

Read each of these arguments about whether access to the Internet should be free. Keep in mind the features of an argument and the power of language. Which argument do you feel is stronger? Why?

Internet Access Should Be Free.

How often do you use the Internet? What do you use it for? People need free Internet access to participate in their communities and complete daily tasks.

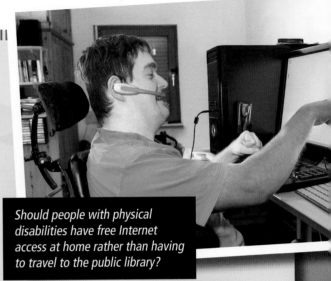

Should people with physical disabilities have free Internet access at home rather than having to travel to the public library?

People need access to the Internet to participate fully in their communities. Information about community events is often posted online only. Many people are required to pay their bills, apply for jobs, and make appointments online. All government departments have websites where information about such things as social services and accessing welfare payments are displayed. It is extremely difficult for people to complete daily tasks or participate in their communities if they cannot afford Internet access at home. In the United States, the minimum cost for Internet access at home is around $35 per month, but it often costs far more. For those who are unemployed or in low-income jobs, being unable to pay this fee can act as an extra barrier to full participation in both the local and wider community.

Some people argue that Internet access should not be free. It is a service, and like any other service, it needs money to maintain it and make it better. For example, every day, dozens of people work to maintain the cables and wires that form the Internet in New York City. They all have to be paid to do their jobs. People argue that paying for the Internet will result in faster Internet access. However, the Internet is not a luxury: It is an essential resource for participation in the worlds of learning, work, and government. If there is a cost to maintaining the Internet, that fee should be paid from **taxes** rather than from the pockets of those who cannot afford it.

In the modern world, the Internet is the main gateway to information. Information should always be free. The Internet must be free for everyone, whatever their income, so that we can all learn, share, and grow together.

People Should Pay for Internet Access.

Was your cell phone free? Are the tickets free when you go to the movies? Just like other forms of communication and entertainment, Internet access must be paid for.

The Internet is made up of wired networks, composed of wires and cables, and wireless networks, composed of **satellite** and Wi-Fi senders and receivers. There is an immense cost to creating and maintaining these networks. An estimate quoted in *Forbes* business magazine put the cost of maintaining the worldwide Internet at $100–$200 billion per year. This cost needs to be paid by Internet users.

Some people argue that the Internet is not like other forms of communication and entertainment. They argue that, in the modern world, access to the Internet is a necessity for daily life, not a luxury like movie tickets. However, the Internet is no more essential than a cell phone or a television, both of which must be paid for. Access to the Internet may be beneficial for learning, but students do have free access to the Internet in classrooms and public libraries. Although some jobs can be applied for online, and some bills can be paid online, there is always the alternative of carrying out these tasks in person or by mail.

Although the Internet has the ability to improve our daily lives, it is not a necessity. Watching YouTube videos and Snapchatting with our friends are not essential to our health. In a fair society, we must all pay for the services we use.

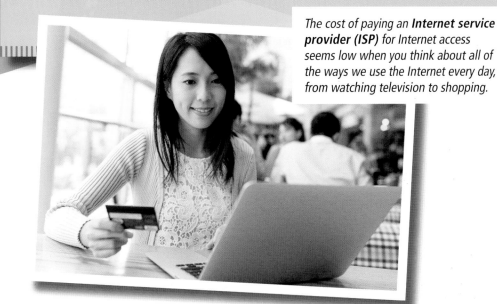

*The cost of paying an **Internet service provider (ISP)** for Internet access seems low when you think about all of the ways we use the Internet every day, from watching television to shopping.*

CHAPTER 3

SHOULD ROBOTS BE ALLOWED TO REPLACE HUMAN WORKERS?

Factories and **manufacturing plants** have been using robots to make cars and other vehicles for decades. Other jobs that use robots and **automated machines** include **warehouses**, **call centers**, delivery services, and grocery store checkouts. Robots may replace many more humans in the workplace in the future. What could be the downside of robots replacing humans in jobs?

Superefficient Robots

Robots can perform many tasks better than humans, particularly those that are **repetitive**, require strength, or are dangerous. For example, in farming, robots plant crops and check entire fields for pests and weeds, whatever the weather. In medicine, robots analyze thousands of test results from patients. They can also do very delicate and exact tasks, such as the measurement of tiny quantities of chemicals.

However, there are some tasks that require humans. Some jobs, such as banking, insurance, or legal work, involve **interaction** between people or

critical thinking. Machines have no emotions or feelings so they also cannot replace humans in jobs that require these human skills. In many jobs, face-to-face interaction is preferred. Although a robot might be able to **diagnose** an illness, many patients are more likely to prefer to be told their results by a doctor or nurse. Yet, even in jobs in which human interaction is important, robots are being used. In the fast food industry, for example, people often make their orders on computer systems. Robots could soon be cooking food in kitchens! And when robots do replace human workers, what might happen to those people when their jobs change or are removed entirely?

Robots are able to do many different kinds of work. They can be used alongside human workers to make some tasks safer or easier.

In some areas of work, robots and humans are likely to work side by side in the future workplace. Robots will do the repetitive tasks, and humans will do work that needs critical thinking or creativity. For example, future robots may build homes, while humans design them and decide which features make them great to live in.

People Are Still Important

There are many tasks that can be done by robots but few jobs that can be completely automated at present. In most cases, a human is needed to operate or **program** a robot. A person also needs to maintain and repair a robot. Although many jobs might be lost by automation, others will be created. By 2025, it is estimated that automation will replace 22.7 million jobs in the United States. In the same period, 13.6 million new jobs will be created. These will be in areas such as design, engineering, maintenance, **software** support, and training.

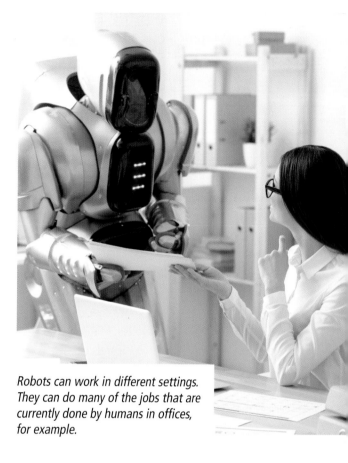

Robots can work in different settings. They can do many of the jobs that are currently done by humans in offices, for example.

So, what are the arguments for and against robots at work?

ROBOTS AND JOBS

Here are some interesting statistics about robots and jobs:

- Up to 5 million jobs in the United States have already been lost to automation and robots.
- According to the McKinsey Global Institute, up to one-third of workers in richer nations, such as Canada and the United States, will need to retrain by 2030, so that they do not lose their jobs to automation.
- By 2024, 80,000 jobs in the United States' fast food industry will be lost to robots and automation, while up to 5 million driver jobs will be lost to driverless vehicles.

Robots Should Be Allowed to Replace Humans in the Workplace.

Robots are stronger, safer, and more reliable than human workers. In 2015, the Japanese robot maker Fanuc set a new world record when its robot lifted 2.5 tons (2.27 metric tons). This is approximately the same weight as an adult rhinoceros. Robots are safer because they can do dangerous jobs that may harm humans. This will reduce the number of humans that might be injured in the workplace. According to General Robert Cone, robots and drones could replace one-quarter of U.S. combat soldiers by 2030, removing human soldiers from harm. Robots will help people explore space, too, by traveling to places too distant and dangerous for humans. The Valkyrie robot is being developed for space exploration by the National Aeronautics and

Space Administration (NASA). It has sophisticated hands for using tools and will one day travel to Mars. Unlike humans, robots do not need breaks or get bored. They can work on repetitive tasks 24 hours a day without stopping. Acieta, which has installed 4,500 robotic systems in factories across the United States, says that its robots allow production lines to run continuously.

Robots are more **versatile** than humans. Robots can be built in many different shapes and sizes. Some have tiny "arms" that enable them to do delicate jobs that humans cannot do. Robots are always carefully designed and built for a specific job. Unlike human workers, they do not need

Large robots are used in factories. By 2019, more than 1.4 million new robots will start work in factories in different parts of the world.

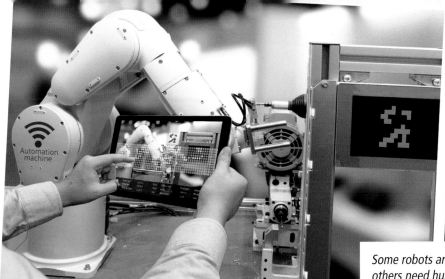

Some robots are fully automated, but others need humans to program or operate them. Safety can be a problem when robots work beside humans.

to be trained. For example, robots can perform delicate surgeries again and again without error. In hospitals around the world in 2016, robots took part in more than 750,000 surgeries. The FarmBot is a mobile robot that sows and feeds crops and controls weeds in the fields, and the robot Flippy was built with flexible arms to prepare burgers in fast-food kitchens.

Some people argue that robots should not replace humans in the workplace. Robots are only reliable if they are in good working order, and machines do break down. If a factory depends on robots to do everything, no work will be completed if the robots are out of service. Robots can also be unsafe. In the United States, since 1984, the Occupational Safety and Health Administration (OSHA) has recorded 38 robot-related accidents, 27 of which resulted in a worker's death.

However, all these accidents involved service robots, working alongside people. Factory robots usually operate inside cages, so they are very safe. The deaths are also a very small percentage of the total number of workplace deaths. There were 4,585 deaths in the U.S. workplace in 2013, the last year that there was a robot-related death. Robots are also improving and becoming more sophisticated all the time, with **sensors** that allow them to detect the presence of a human and immediately stop work. Any issues with safety or reliability will become fewer in the future as more robots enter the workplace.

Due to the benefits that robot workers bring to the workplace, they should be allowed to replace human workers. They are more efficient than humans in many ways and can keep people safer by handling more dangerous jobs.

Robots Should Not Be Allowed to Replace Humans in the Workplace.

Robots should not replace humans in jobs because they will strip people of their livelihoods. They are also unreliable and cannot replace important human skills. The number of robots in the United States is expected to quadruple by 2025. This will lead to the loss of between 1.9 and 3.4 million jobs across the country. People go to work to earn money, so that they can pay for housing, food, and other necessities. Without jobs, people will not have the money they need to support themselves and their families. Not everyone will be able to take advantage of new jobs related to robot design, programming, and maintenance. It costs money to attend school to learn new skills, and many people cannot afford the expense. From 2017 to 2018, the average cost to attend university or college in the U.S. was more than $20,000. Some older workers may not have the ability to change their career quickly, if they lose their job to a robot. A study in 2010 by Boston College learned that 41 percent of older workers were seen as resistant to change, and 34 percent were reluctant to use new technology at work.

Around 70 percent of industrial robots are currently used in the automotive, electrical/electronics, and metal and machinery industries. As a result, jobs for people have decreased in these industries.

Since robots are machines, they are likely to break down over time. They require humans to monitor, maintain, and repair them. When one robot breaks down, it could harm a whole production line, since it will have to be repaired before work can resume. Companies will need to spend more money on training people to work with robots and repair them if they break. Robots can be programmed to do certain repetitive jobs, but they cannot deal with unexpected situations. They cannot solve any problems that may arise. Dr. Tom Hoyland at Hull University Business School in the UK believes that robots can never fill every role in a business effectively, as humans will always be needed to provide new, creative ideas: "Technology cannot replicate the chance meeting within the organization where chitchat unveils common problems or builds linkages."

Some say that the use of robots in the workplace will mean that new, different jobs will be created for humans and that these jobs will be highly qualified positions that have higher pay. If robots do break down sometimes, well-skilled humans will need to fix them. "This is the evolution of the repair person. It's harder to fix a robot than it is to fix a vending machine," says technology analyst J. P. Gownder. However, the number of jobs lost to robots will not be replaced by an equal number of jobs in robot maintenance and design. A 2017 report by the McKinsey Global Institute, which has offered advice to global businesses for 90 years, states that, by 2030, up to 800 million jobs will be lost worldwide to automation. There are not enough new jobs to replace those lost.

Robot workers should not be allowed to replace human workers, as this will lead to job losses, particularly among older workers and those who cannot afford to train as programmers, designers, or inventors. Robots can be unreliable. They are still machines and will need humans to operate and repair them.

Although robots are more efficient in many ways, humans are still required. People may still need to check over a robot's work to make sure that it has been done correctly.

STATE YOUR CASE

When it comes to any issue, you need to look at arguments on both sides before you decide where you stand. When you evaluate the arguments for and against robot workers, remember the features of effective arguments. Which side's argument do you think is stronger? Why do you think so? Give reasons for your answers. Use the "In Summary: For and Against" list to help you figure out your decision, and state your own case.

IN SUMMARY: FOR AND AGAINST

For Robot Workers

Robot workers are safer, more reliable, and stronger than human workers.

- The Japanese robot maker Fanuc has a robot that can lift 2.5 tons (2.27 metric tons).
- Robots work with dangerous materials such as chemicals, helping to reduce human injuries in the workplace. Robots could also replace one-quarter of U.S. combat soldiers by 2030, reducing the risk to human soldiers.
- NASA's Valkyrie robot is being developed for space exploration, so that humans can discover distant and dangerous places.
- Robots do not need breaks or get bored, and can work on certain tasks 24 hours a day.

Robot workers are more versatile than humans.

- Some robots have tiny parts, enabling them to complete delicate jobs that humans cannot do. Robotic surgeons can perform some operations better than human doctors.
- Robots can be built in many different shapes and sizes and with moving parts specially adapted for specific jobs.
- Robots do not need to be trained for a job like human workers.

In the United States, vehicle production has increased by 16 percent every year since 2010. This is mostly a result of industrial robots working more efficiently.

Against Robot Workers

Robots will leave many humans without the jobs they need to support themselves.

- The number of robots in the United States will quadruple by 2025, resulting in the loss of between 1.9 and 3.4 million jobs.
- People who lose their jobs will have no money to spend on the things they need to live.
- Some people cannot afford to pay for training in skills such as robot programming and design.
- Some older workers may not have the ability to retrain in different roles.

Robots are not completely reliable because they could break down, and they need humans to program, control, and maintain them.

- Since robots are machines, they are likely to break down, resulting in the stoppage of production lines.
- Robots can only be programmed to do certain repetitive jobs.
- Robots cannot deal with unexpected situations.
- Robots cannot think for themselves to solve new problems.
- Robots can never fill every role in a business effectively, as humans will always be needed to supply new ideas.

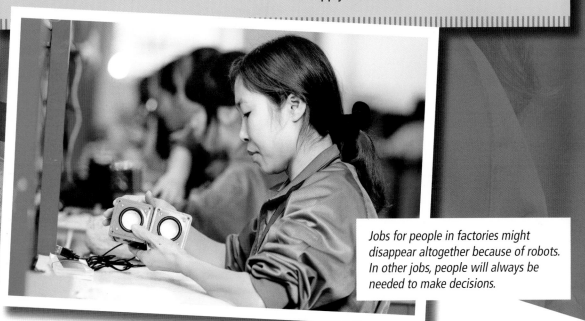

Jobs for people in factories might disappear altogether because of robots. In other jobs, people will always be needed to make decisions.

CHAPTER 4

SHOULD VEHICLES BE DRIVERLESS IN THE FUTURE?

A large number of driverless vehicles will be on the roads in the coming decades. By 2020, vehicle manufacturers Toyota and Nissan expect to have produced vehicles that can access a highway, drive through a busy city, and change lanes without action by a driver. Are driverless cars the future? Are there any drawbacks to driverless vehicles?

Change on the Roads

Cars that are fully automated control all the car's functions, from steering and acceleration to braking and swerving to avoid obstacles. They use cameras and sensors to detect other vehicles, traffic lights, and changes in weather. If the technology of driverless cars continues to improve, people may stop wanting to own a vehicle that they drive themselves. Automobile giants Ford and BMW expect to have some driverless car models by 2021, so the number of driverless cars on the roads is likely to increase steeply during the 2020s. This will reduce the possibilities for human error, which often causes accidents resulting in loss of life, injury, and traffic congestion.

The technology used in driverless cars is very sophisticated. It could allow the "driver" to do other things, such as read, on their journey.

Most of the driverless cars currently in development are powered by electricity, not gasoline or diesel. Some are **hybrids** and are powered by both electric batteries and a gasoline engine. These cars are better for the environment than those that burn gasoline and diesel. However, although driverless cars are programmed to avoid pedestrians that might step into their path unexpectedly, there are concerns that a driverless car might not be able to take action as quickly as a human driver.

Driverless Truck Convoys

The automated trucking company Otto, based in San Francisco, aims to have a large number of driverless trucks on the road in the next ten years. There are already teams of driverless trucks at work in enclosed locations, such as ports and construction sites. Sometimes a driverless truck has an operator in the cab. But at other times, a **convoy** of trucks has a person in just one of the vehicles who works as the operator—or the operator is at another location, such as a port control tower. In the future, convoys of driverless trucks may progress down major highways like

trains. If the trucks drive close together on the highway, they will save fuel because there will be less **wind drag**.

Self-driving trucks have several cameras and sensors, some of which are on top of the cab, giving an excellent high-level view of traffic up ahead. In the cab, there is a very powerful computer that controls the truck's steering, braking, and other systems. A person can also press a button beside the steering wheel at any time to take over from the self-driving system.

In October 2018, a truck with Otto's equipment drove itself along a highway in Colorado. A person sat in the truck during the journey in case of an emergency, but did not touch the controls. However, it could still be a while before entirely driverless trucks are commonplace on the highway. "We're at least a decade away from having a truck with no driver in it," says Otto's Eric Berdinis.

So, what are the arguments for and against driverless vehicles?

This electricity-powered driverless bus was tested in Paris, France. In the future, every bus may be driverless.

Vehicles Should Be Driverless in the Future.

Vehicles should be driverless because they are safer and more efficient, or they are able to complete a job quickly and effectively. There will be far fewer accidents if all cars are driverless. More than 90 percent of vehicle crashes in the United States are the fault of the driver. Around 30,000 Americans and 2,000 Canadians die in car accidents every year. Distracted driving is the cause of 10 percent of these deaths. These accidents would not happen if vehicles were automated. "Society tolerates a significant amount of human error on our roads," says Gill Pratt of Toyota's Research Institute. "We are, after all, only human. On the other hand, we expect machines to perform much better." According to Shai Magzimof of Phantom Auto driverless

car systems, driverless vehicles can still allow a person to take control when required. This may include harsh weather conditions, or problems on the road that need a human operator, such as when a traffic police officer is using hand signals.

Driverless cars are more efficient. It is possible to program driverless cars so that they always obey the speed limit and the rules of the road. When every car follows road rules, traffic will flow more smoothly. They can also be programmed to keep a steady speed, which improves energy efficiency. People will be able to sleep or work while they are on a journey. If they become sick while driving, they can turn on the vehicle's self-driving function. "Some computers now have perception at levels of competence close to what a human has," says Gill Pratt, head of the Toyota Research Institute. He says that driverless cars can now tell the difference between a bicycle and a person walking, or between a tree and a parking meter—and then can act on what they see at least as well as a human being.

Some people believe that cars should not be driverless. There have already been accidents when these cars have been tested. According to

Tired drivers will have the option for their vehicle to drive itself. This will reduce the number of accidents caused by driver fatigue.

John M. Simpson, privacy and technology project director with **Consumer Watchdog**, "The robot cars cannot accurately predict human behavior, and the real problem comes in the interaction between humans and the robot vehicles." However, human drivers make mistakes such as running red lights, endangering themselves and other drivers. Driverless cars never make these reckless choices. Driverless cars and trucks are still a work in progress, and fully automated vehicles will not be allowed on public highways until they are entirely safe. With the speed at which this technology is progressing, any remaining safety issues will soon be resolved.

All vehicles should be driverless because they are more efficient and safer than human drivers. When all cars on the highway are fully automated, no more lives will be lost by human error behind the wheel.

Some apps may allow us to call for a driverless cab when we need one. This will be more convenient for many people.

Vehicles Should Not Be Driverless in the Future.

Driverless vehicles should not replace cars with human drivers. They cannot replace human thought and are not safer in many situations. They could also cause people to lose jobs. Driverless vehicles are not safe for drivers or pedestrians. Although driverless vehicles have cameras and sensors to detect pedestrians, changing traffic lights, or swerving bicycles, sensors may react more slowly in bad weather. Like all mechanical equipment, this technology may eventually fail altogether, resulting in dangerous accidents. Driverless cars have had accidents during testing. In March 2018, a pedestrian was hit and killed by a driverless car in Arizona. The car had a human operator, but was driving on its own when the accident happened. According to Shai Magzimof of Phantom Auto driverless car systems, "unidentified objects" such as plastic bags fluttering into the road or dump trucks making a sudden turn from a construction site "can be hard" for driverless vehicles. It is when the unexpected happens that safety is a major concern for driverless cars. Until all safety issues are resolved, there are likely to be accidents with driverless cars.

People who drive vehicles for a living will lose their jobs if vehicles are driverless. Millions of driver jobs will be lost to driverless vehicles. This will include jobs at taxi, trucking, and delivery companies. In the United States in 2014, there were 4 million driver jobs. It is estimated that up to 5 million driver jobs will be lost to driverless vehicles in the 2020s.

Driverless vehicles pose many safety challenges in major cities. The technology will need to improve to make sure that pedestrians and other drivers are safe.

Some people argue that driverless cars are safer as computers are never distracted, unlike human drivers. However, there are too many situations, such as bad weather, when a driverless car may become far more dangerous than an ordinary car. For example, according to Wireless Design and Development, in heavy snow, a driverless car's sensors cannot tell the snow from lane markings.

Vehicles should not be driverless in the future because sensors and computers will never be as safe as a human who can react with all their intelligence and experience regarding unexpected events on the road. Driverless vehicles will also lead to the loss of too many jobs.

There are many things that could cause driverless vehicles to have accidents. Will driverless vehicles ever be completely safe?

STATE YOUR CASE

When it comes to any issue, you need to look at arguments on both sides before you decide where you stand. When you think about arguments for and against driverless vehicles, remember the features of effective arguments. Which argument do you think is the strongest? Why do you think that one side is more powerful than the other? Give reasons for your answers. Use the "In Summary: For and Against" list to help you figure out your decision, and state your own case.

IN SUMMARY: FOR AND AGAINST

For Driverless Cars

Driverless vehicles are safer.

- There will be fewer accidents if all cars are driverless because accidents are often caused by human error. Distracted driving is the cause of 10 percent of the deaths in car accidents in the United States and Canada.
- Driverless vehicles can still allow a person to take control in an emergency or harsh weather conditions.

Driverless cars are more efficient.

- People will be able to sleep or work while they are on a journey.
- Driverless cars can be programmed to be more energy efficient by keeping a steady speed.
- Since all driverless cars are programmed to obey road rules, there will be a smoother flow of traffic.

Roads will be safer if cars become driverless. The technology that they use will help protect other road users and pedestrians alike.

Against Driverless Cars

Driverless vehicles are not safe for drivers or pedestrians.

- Driverless cars have had accidents during testing. In March 2018, a pedestrian was hit and killed by a driverless car in Arizona.
- Driverless cars can be affected by poor weather conditions that might cause the cameras and sensors not to work properly.
- Driverless cars are entirely reliant on technology and so could possibly malfunction.
- Driverless cars have difficulty identifying unusual objects, such as fluttering plastic bags.

People who drive for a living will lose their jobs if vehicles are driverless.

- Millions of driver jobs in taxi, trucking, and delivery companies will be lost to driverless vehicles.
- Up to 5 million driver jobs in the United States could be lost to driverless vehicles in the 2020s.
- Older drivers will find it particularly difficult to find jobs in a different industry.

Towns and cities are full of people. The technology may never be good enough to ensure that driverless vehicles can always react to other drivers and pedestrians.

CHAPTER 5

SHOULD YOUNG PEOPLE HAVE ACCESS TO ALL TECHNOLOGY, ALL THE TIME?

Today, computers, laptops, and cell phones are used by just about everyone in the United States, including many children and teenagers. Some people argue that we are all better connected and better informed as a result of the constant access we have to technology. However, others are concerned that young people have too much access to technology.

We use social media sites such as Facebook every day, take photos with our phones and share them on Instagram, play video and online computer games, write and read blogs on sites such as Tumblr, and use our phones and other devices to pinpoint our locations or to locate other people and businesses. We also use wearable technology, such as Apple Watches or Fitbits. Technology is such a major part of our daily lives that it is hard to imagine life without it.

Tech Troubles

There are concerns that young people should not have access to all technology, all the time. Some people fear that children and teenagers might become too dependent on technology. This could lead to less social interaction with other young people. Some families are not able to afford the latest gadgets, which could lead to issues at school or in social settings for those from low-income families. There are also concerns about what children might be viewing online. The Internet has a wealth of information to help learning, but some websites are inappropriate for a younger audience. Violence shown in videos and in games might also be harmful. Young people do not get as much exercise or go outside as often if they spend too much time on electronic gadgets. This will make them less healthy.

Not All Bad

Some technology is beneficial and has improved our lives. Social media allows us to stay in touch with our friends and family and connect with people who live far away. Blogs and similar online platforms have given us ways to express ourselves and showcase our creativity. Social media such as Facebook and Twitter have also been very important for activism in recent years. Social media campaigns have allowed people to raise awareness about important issues in society and organize protest marches or petitions. For example, in 2017, the Me Too movement against harassment of women spread globally through Twitter.

Young people have grown up with technology and use it to keep in touch. Millions of images are taken and uploaded to websites every day.

In 2014, the ice bucket challenge used social media to raise awareness of the disease amyotrophic lateral sclerosis (ALS). Videos of people tipping buckets of cold water over their heads during the campaign raised more than $100 million for charity.

Technology such as laptops and tablets is common in classrooms. Some schools have adopted virtual libraries instead of printed books, resulting in more information from a wider range of sources being available. In **distance learning**, the Internet and accessible devices have allowed children to learn online when they are too unwell to attend school. Home schooling has also greatly benefited from technology, since it increases access to information and online learning tools.

Young people use their electronic devices for learning as well as for entertainment.

So, what are the arguments for and against access to technology?

YOUNG PEOPLE AND TECHNOLOGY

Take a look at these statistics about young people and technology:

- In the United States, teenagers spend up to 11 hours a day looking at a screen.
- Nearly 100 percent of young Canadians age 15 to 24 use the Internet every day or have their own smartphone.
- In the United States, 73 percent of teenagers age 13 to 17 own smartphones.
- By age 8, more than 80 percent of children in North America have played console video games, and 60 percent have used apps or played games on a handheld device.
- More than 75 percent of Canadians age 15 to 34 use the Internet to follow news and current affairs online.

Young People Should Have Access to All Technology, All the Time.

It is important for children to have access to all types of technology, all the time, because of the benefits technology provides to learning and personal relationships. Technology is essential to a young person's learning. Young people need access to technology to access information online and to keep up-to-date with world events. Children can learn more about people in other countries if they have access to the Internet. In some cases, using a computer is the only way they can now find information, as libraries often keep some materials, such as encyclopedias, digitally. Children who have trouble learning in a mainstream school, such as learners who have physical disabilities, can learn online instead. This would not be possible without unrestricted access to technology and computers. Schools are already very dependent on technology, and they are likely to become more so. If children and teenagers do not have access to the latest technology, they will not be able to take part in classes. In the United States, 98 percent of schools have more than one computer in the classroom; 84 percent of schools have high-speed Internet; and 77 percent of teachers use the Internet for instruction. Technology is giving access not just to more information, but to whole new ways of learning, says David Goodrum, director of academic technology and information services at Oregon State University.

Children become familiar with technology at a young age. They not only use it in their social lives, but also at school.

Many young people rely on technology in their education. This means that they have all the tools they need for learning.

Technology allows young people to interact with friends and family. Through technology such as e-mail, Skype, and FaceTime, young people can stay in contact with friends and family who live far away. Before the invention of such instant and low-cost technologies, long-distance communication was slow, via letter, or expensive, via phone calls. Having access to social media and other online platforms can also bring together people with similar interests, such as in history or animation. In 2015, a study by the Pew Research Center found that 57 percent of teens age 13 to 17 have made new friends online.

Some people believe that young people should not have access to all technology, all the time, as spending too much time with phones, computers, and laptops means that they are spending less time interacting in person. Too much screen time can also cause health problems, such as straining a young person's eyesight. However, young people who are shy or struggle to interact in person can form links with others online. And although excessive screen time can cause eyestrain, this can be resolved by taking breaks. Dr. Christopher Starr, associate professor of ophthalmology at Weill Cornell Medicine in New York, explains that eye strain can be reduced by taking breaks from screen time.

Young people need access to all technology, all the time, so that they can be well educated and well informed. In many schools and colleges, they would be unable to do their classwork or homework without access to technology. Young people also need technology to stay in contact with friends and family, and to pursue their interests.

Young People Should Not Have Access to All Technology, All the Time.

Constant access to technology harms social interactions and causes health problems in young people. It should not be easily accessible all the time. Spending too much time online with games and social media can cause young people to become isolated from their peers, and lose some of the face-to-face communication skills they need. Some young people suffer from **cyberbullying**. Cyberbullying is bullying that takes place online, such as on social media. Victims of cyberbullying describe feeling like there is no escape, because of the ongoing attacks they experience through digital devices at home and at school, at all times of day. If access to technology is restricted, cyberbullying is less pervasive, or ongoing. Around 43 percent of children and teens say that they have been bullied online. In addition, 81 percent of children and teens believe it is easier to be a bully online than it is in person.

Unrestricted access to technology can cause health problems. Too much screen time can strain the eyes. Children should have restricted screen time to prevent long-term damage to their eyesight.

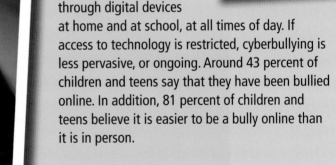

Limiting access to technology would help prevent health issues in young people, as well as problems with social interaction.

Cyberbullying is much harder for teachers and parents to notice, so it's harder to help stop it. Cyberbullying can be very frightening for many young people.

Vancouver optometrist Dr. Mini Randhawa believes that too much screen time is leading to more nearsightedness in children, whose eyes keep developing until they are around 20 years old. "The problem with screen time is it actually has some pretty significant side effects on our eyes, particularly kids' eyes," she says. Too much screen time, such as playing video games, can also negatively affect children's health. Children who do not get enough exercise can develop **obesity** and other health problems. Video games can also affect a child's ability to concentrate on one task for a longer period of time. In 2010, a study published in the medical journal *Pediatrics* found that elementary school children who play video

games for more than two hours a day are 67 percent more likely than their peers who play less to have greater-than-average attention problems.

Some people argue that technology allows young people to stay connected with peers and family members who they might not see very often. Some young people also find it easier to interact online than in person. However, spending too much time online is damaging the social skills of young people. Some find it difficult to interact in person, which affects their performance in situations such as job interviews once they have finished their education. A 2016 report by King's College London, in England, questioned more than 200 businesses. These businesses said they wasted an increasing amount of time interviewing young people who had very poor social skills.

Young people should not have access to all technology at all times because it results in them becoming isolated from their peers, makes them vulnerable to cyberbullying, and damages their social skills. It also damages their eyesight and prevents them from exercising.

STATE YOUR CASE

When it comes to any issue, you need to look at arguments on both sides before you decide where you stand. Remember the features of effective arguments when you think about arguments for and against young people having access to all technology, all the time. Which argument do you think is the most convincing? Why do you think that one is better than the other? Give reasons for your answers. Use the "In Summary: For and Against" list to help you figure out your decision, and state your own case.

IN SUMMARY: FOR AND AGAINST

For Young People Having Access to Technology All the Time

Technology is essential to a young person's learning.

- Young people need technology to access information online to complete school projects and stay well informed.
- Children need Internet access to learn more about the lives and perspectives of different people.
- Computers are increasingly common in classrooms, so children and teenagers will need access to the latest technology to take part in classes at school.
- Children that have difficulty learning in a mainstream school, such as learners with disabilities, can learn online.

Technology allows young people to interact with friends and family.

- Technology allows children and teenagers to stay in contact with friends and family who live far away.
- Technology has increased the speed and reduced the cost of long-distance communication.
- Social media allows people with similar interests to connect with each other.
- 57 percent of teens age 13 to 17 have made new friends online.

Many jobs in the future will depend on knowledge of technology. Isn't it important for young people to be prepared for their future careers?

Against Young People Having Access to Technology All the Time

Constant access to technology harms social interactions for young people.

- Spending too much time online with games and social media can cause some young people to become isolated from their peers.
- Some young people suffer from cyberbullying.
- Excessive use of technology means that some young people are not acquiring social skills. This could lead to them having problems with interviews and in the workplace.

Unrestricted access to technology can cause health problems.

- Children should have restricted screen time to keep them from damaging their eyesight.
- Excessive video gaming can reduce a child's ability to concentrate.
- Children and teenagers who spend too much time indoors with technology do not get enough exercise, which can lead to obesity and other health problems.

People still need to talk to each other in person, socially and in the workplace. Restricted access to technology will help to preserve their social skills.

BIBLIOGRAPHY

Technology Today and Tomorrow

"How Technology Affects Your Social Skills." Liberty Classical Academy. http://libertyclassicalacademy.org/technology-affects-social-skills

Patterson, Christina. "Our Teenagers Need Social Skills, Not Social Networks." *The Guardian,* March 22, 2016. www.theguardian.com/commentisfree/2016/mar/22/teenagers-social-skills-not-social-networks-work-ncs

Woda, Steven. "Teens and Social Media: Are Social Skills Slipping?" UKnowKids, November 19, 2014. http://resources.uknowkids.com/blog/teens-and-social-media-are-social-skills-slipping

What Makes an Argument?

"4.6 Billion People Live without Internet Access." A Human Right, 2018. http://ahumanright.org

"Buy an E-Book Save a Tree—Are E-Readers Better for the Environment?" FilterBuy https://filterbuy.com/buy-ebook-save-tree-ereaders-better-environment

"Constructing an Argument." Massey University, February 8, 2018. http://owll.massey.ac.nz/study-skills/constructing-an-argument.php

Doyne, Shannon. "Would You Trade Your Paper Books for Digital Versions?" The *New York Times,* October 21, 2010. https://learning.blogs.nytimes.com/2010/10/21/would-you-trade-your-paper-books-for-digital-versions

"E-Books in the Elementary Classroom: Benefits of E-Books." University of Ontario, Institute of Technology, November 8, 2016. http://guides.library.uoit.ca/c.php?g=33133&p=210168

"Examples of Ethos, Logos, and Pathos." Your Dictionary. http://examples.yourdictionary.com/examples-of-ethos-logos-and-pathos.html

Gallagher, James. "E-Books 'Damage Sleep and Health,' Doctors Warn." *BBC News,* December 23, 2014. http://www.bbc.com/news/health-30574260

Girard, Patrick. "What Are Arguments?" Future Learn, University of Auckland. www.futurelearn.com/courses/logical-and-critical-thinking/0/steps/9137

Gonchar, Michael. "200 Prompts for Argumentative Writing." *The New York Times,* February 4, 2014. https://learning.blogs.nytimes.com/2014/02/04/200-prompts-for-argumentative-writing

Internet World Stats: Usage and population statistics. www.internetworldstats.com/stats.htm

Murray, Jacqui. "13 Reasons for Using Technology in the Classroom." TeachHub. www.teachhub.com/13-reasons-using-technology-classroom

"Print vs. Digital: Which Is Better for Your Eyesight?" Vision Source, January 13, 2016. http://visionsource.com/blog/print-vs-digital-which-is-better-for-your-eyesight

Puiu, Tibi. "Overwhelming Majority of College Students Prefer Paper Books to Digital Copies." ZME Science, January 15, 2015. www.zmescience.com/research/technology/people-prefer-books-over-ebook-042432

Roberts, Jennifer. "Computers in Classroom Have 'Mixed' Impact on Learning: OECD Report." The *Globe and Mail,* March 25, 2017. www.theglobeandmail.com/news/national/education/computers-in-classroom-have-mixed-impact-on-learning-oecd-report/article26373533

Schulten, Katherine. "10 Ways to Teach Argument-Writing with *The New York Times.*" *The New York Times,* October 5, 2017. www.nytimes.com/2017/10/05/learning/lesson-plans/10-ways-to-teach-argument-writing-with-the-new-york-times.html

Street, Elizabeth. "How Laptops in the Classroom Improve Student Learning." Learning Liftoff, January 24, 2017. www.learningliftoff.com/how-laptops-in-the-classroom-improve-student-learning

"The Great Debate: Print Books vs. E-Books." Reading Eggs, May 29, 2015. https://blog.readingeggs.com/2015/05/29/the-great-debate-print-books-vs-e-books

"The Impact of ebooks on the Reading Motivation and Reading Skills of Children and Young People." National Literacy Trust, December 9, 2015. https://literacytrust.org.uk/research-services/research-reports/impact-ebooks-reading-motivation-and-reading-skills-children-and-young-people

Tower, Anna. "What Is the Clincher at the End of Your Essay?" Pen & the Pad, June 13, 2017. https://penandthepad.com/clincher-end-essay-3995.html

Weida, Stacy, and Karl Stolley. "Using Rhetorical Devices for Persuasion." Purdue Online Writing Lab, March 11, 2013. https://owl.english.purdue.edu/owl/resource/588/04

"What Is an E-Book? And 8 Reasons You Should Read Them." TCK Publishing. www.tckpublishing.com/what-is-an-ebook

"What Is Argument?" AEGEE Europe, June 5, 2014. www.zeus.aegee.org/debate/what-is-argument

Should Robots Be Allowed to Replace Human Workers?

Atherton, Kelsey. "Robots May Replace One-Fourth Of U.S. Combat Soldiers By 2030, Says General." *Popular Science,* January 22, 2014. https://www.popsci.com/article/technology/robots-may-replace-one-fourth-us-combat-soldiers-2030-says-general

Cox, Laura. "10 Jobs Where Robots Really Are Replacing Humans." Disruption, May 16, 2017. https://disruptionhub.com/10-jobs-robots-replacing-humans

"Dangerous Robot Jobs." Robotics Online, November 15, 2016. www.robotics.org/blog-article.cfm/Dangerous-Robot-Jobs/15

Gownder, J. P. "Robots Will Transform, Not Replace, Human Work." *Computer Weekly,* January 2016. www.computerweekly.com/opinion/Robots-will-transform-not-replace-human-work

Hill, Catey. "10 Jobs Robots Already Do Better Than You." MarketWatch, June 30, 2017. www.marketwatch.com/story/9-jobs-robots-already-do-better-than-you-2014-01-27

Kessler, Sarah. "The Optimist's Guide to the Robot Apocalypse." Quartz Media, March 9, 2017. https://qz.com/904285/the-optimists-guide-to-the-robot-apocalypse

Onibalusi, Lanre. "5 Reasons Why Robots Will Never Fully Replace Humans." Tech.Co, August 2, 2017. https://tech.co/robots-replace-humans-work-2017-08

McFarland, Matt. "Robots: Is Your Job at Risk?" CNN Tech, September 15, 2017. http://money.cnn.com/2017/09/15/technology/jobs-robots/index.html

Metz, Cade. "Robots Will Steal Our Jobs, but They'll Give Us New Ones." *Wired,* August 24, 2015. https://www.wired.com/2015/08/robots-will-steal-jobs-theyll-give-us-new-ones

"New Surgical Robots Are about to Enter the Operating Theatre." The *Economist,* November 16, 2017. www.economist.com/news/science-and-technology/21731378-surgeons-will-soon-have-more-helping-mechanical-hands-new-surgical-robots-are

Nichols, Greg. "Robots Are Coming to Work. Are They Safe?" ZDNet, October 10, 2017. https://www.zdnet.com/article/robots-are-coming-to-work-are-they-safe

Rendall, Matthew. "Industrial Robots Will Replace Manufacturing Jobs—and That's a Good Thing." Tech Crunch, October 9, 2016 https://techcrunch.com/2016/10/09/industrial-robots-will-replace-manufacturing-jobs-and-thats-a-good-thing

Shewan, Dan. "Robots Will Destroy Our Jobs—and We're Not Ready for It." *The Guardian*, January 11, 2017. www.theguardian.com/technology/2017/jan/11/robots-jobs-employees-artificial-intelligence

Stark, Harold. "As Robots Rise, How Artificial Intelligence Will Impact Jobs." *Forbes*, April 28, 2017. www.forbes.com/sites/haroldstark/2017/04/28/as-robots-rise-how-artificial-intelligence-will-impact-jobs/#eebf5507687d

"'World's Strongest' Robot Can Lift 2.3 Tonnes." Drives & Controls, October 8, 2015. http://drivesncontrols.com/news/fullstory.php/aid/4923/_91World_92s_strongest_92_robot_can_lift_2.3_tonnes.html

Should Vehicles Be Driverless in the Future?

Balakrishnan, Anita. "Self-Driving Cars Could Cost America's Professional Drivers up to 25,000 Jobs a Month." *CNBC*, May 22, 2017. www.cnbc.com/2017/05/22/goldman-sachs-analysis-of-autonomous-vehicle-job-loss.html

Bubbers, Matt, and Chittley, Jordan. "The Future of Mobility." *The Globe and Mail*, November 12, 2017. www.theglobeandmail.com/globe-drive/self-driving-cars-are-going-to-dramatically-change-our-world-so-when-does-the-revolution-begin/article32650833

Davies, Alex. "The Numbers Don't Lie: Self-Driving Cars Are Getting Good." *Wired*, February 2017. www.wired.com/2017/02/california-dmv-autonomous-car-disengagement

Donath, Judith. "Driverless Cars Could Make Transportation Free for Everyone—with a Catch." *The Atlantic*, December 22, 2017. www.theatlantic.com/technology/archive/2017/12/self-driving-cars-free-future/548945

Freedman, David. "Self-Driving Trucks," *MIT Technology Review*, 2017. https://www.technologyreview.com/s/603493/10-breakthrough-technologies-2017-self-driving-trucks

Hancock, Peter. "Are Autonomous Cars Really Safer Than Human Drivers?" *Scientific American*, February 3, 2018. www.scientificamerican.com/article/are-autonomous-cars-really-safer-than-human-drivers

Kessler, Sarah. "A Timeline of When Self-Driving Cars Will Be on the Road, According to the People Making Them." Quartz Media, March 29, 2017. https://qz.com/943899/a-timeline-of-when-self-driving-cars-will-be-on-the-road-according-to-the-people-making-them

Lev, Sam, and Julia Carrie Wong. "Self-Driving Uber Kills Arizona Woman in First Fatal Crash Involving Pedestrian." *The Guardian*, March 19, 2018. https://www.theguardian.com/technology/2018/mar/19/uber-self-driving-car-kills-woman-arizona-tempe

Moldrich, Curtis. "Driverless Cars of the Future: How Far Away Are We from Autonomous Cars?" Alphr, August 7, 2017. www.alphr.com/cars/1001329/driverless-cars-of-the-future-how-far-away-are-we-from-autonomous-cars

Moon, Brad. "First Self-Driving Car Fatality Will Be a Test for the Entire Industry." Investor Place, March 20, 2018. https://investorplace.com/2018/03/first-self-driving-car-fatality-will-test

Naughton, John. "How Driverless Cars Could Change Our Whole Future." *The Guardian*, September 25, 2105. https://www.theguardian.com/commentisfree/2016/sep/25/uber-self-driving-cars-pittsburgh-how-driverless-cars-could-change-our-future-lyft-john-zimmer

Reese, Hope. "Our Autonomous Future: How Driverless Cars Will Be the First Robots We Learn to Trust." TechRepublic, 2017. www.techrepublic.com/article/our-autonomous-future-how-driverless-cars-will-be-the-first-robots-we-learn-to-trust

Shaw, Jerry. "Global Warming: Six Ways Electric Cars Are Better for the Environment." *Newsmax*, March 22, 2015. www.newsmax.com/fastfeatures/cars-global-warming-electric-cars/2015/03/23/id/631734

Should Young People Have Access to All Technology , All the Time?

"A Portrait of Canadian Youth." Statistics Canada, February 7, 2018. https://www.statcan.gc.ca/pub/11-631-x/11-631-x2018001-eng.htm

Bambenek, Cadence. "Facts about Today's Teens' Technology, Social Media Use, and Sex." *Business Insider*, June 29, 2016. www.businessinsider.com/teen-technology-use-2016-6

Chen, Stephanie. "In a Wired World, Children Unable to Escape Cyberbullying." *CNN*, October 5, 2010. http://www.cnn.com/2010/LIVING/10/04/youth.cyberbullying.abuse/index.html

Conrad, Brent. "Media Statistics—Children's Use of TV, Internet, and Video Games." TechAddiction. www.techaddiction.ca/media-statistics.html

Feiler, Bruce. "When Tech Is a Problem Child." *The New York Times*, November 19, 2017. www.nytimes.com/2016/11/20/fashion/children-technology-limits-smartphones.html

Himmelsbach, Vawn. "6 Pros & Cons of Technology in the Classroom in 2018." Top Hat, 2017. https://tophat.com/blog/6-pros-cons-technology-classroom

Lenhart, Amanda. "Teens, Social Media & Technology Overview 2015." Pew Research Center, April 9, 2015. www.pewinternet.org/2015/04/09/teens-social-media-technology-2015

Maps, Professor Andrew Martin. "How Technology Affects Children's Learning." Psychlopaedia, November 17, 2017. https://psychlopaedia.org/learning-and-development/technology-affects-childrens-learning

Patel, Dhruvin. "Will Technology Ruin Your Children's Development?" Thrive Global, March 4, 2017. https://journal.thriveglobal.com/will-technology-ruin-your-childrens-development-663351c76974

Patterson, Christina. "Our Teenagers Need Social Skills, Not Social Networks." *The Guardian*, March 22, 2015. www.theguardian.com/commentisfree/2016/mar/22/teenagers-social-skills-not-social-networks-work-ncs

Raidt, Kate. "Cyberbullying: No Escape?" Advantage4Parents. https://www.advantage4parents.com/article/cyberbullying-no-escape

Rowan, Cris. "The Impact of Technology on the Developing Child." *The Huffington Post*, December 6, 2017. www.huffingtonpost.com/cris-rowan/technology-children-negative-impact_b_3343245.html

Seidman, Bianca. "What Too Much Screen Time Does to Your Eyes." *CBS News*, August 13, 2015. https://www.cbsnews.com/news/screen-time-digital-eye-strain

"Technology and Computers in Classroom Statistics." Statistic Brain, July 3, 2017. https://www.statisticbrain.com/technology-computers-in-classroom-statistics

Zeidler, Maryse. "Too Much Screen Time Could Harm Children's Eyesight, Specialists Warn." *CBC News,* Oct 01, 2017.

GLOSSARY

Please note: Some **boldfaced** words are defined where they appear in the text.

3-D printers Computer-controlled machines that join materials to create an object that is three-dimensional. Three-dimensional objects appear to have length, width, and depth.

artificial intelligence (AI) The ability of a machine to copy intelligent human behavior

audience Spectators, listeners, or readers

automated machines Mechanical devices operated without continuous action by a human being

automation The use of robots and other machines that work without human control in a factory or other workplace

call centers Offices where an organization's telephone transactions take place

code To write programs for a computer

Consumer Watchdog An organization that watches over safety and fairness in areas such as health care, transportation, and politics

convoy A group of vehicles traveling together

critical thinking Evaluating something so as to form an opinion or judgement on it

credible Believable or convincing

cyberbullying Harassing someone online by sending or posting insulting messages or images

diagnose Recognize a disease or injury from its symptoms

disabilities Physical or mental conditions that may affect a person's movement, senses, or activities

distance learning When students receive instruction by mail, online, or by video, instead of going to school

driverless cars Motor vehicles that can be driven by a computer without human control

drones Unmanned aircraft that are guided by remote control or onboard computers

epidemics When diseases, such as the flu or measles, are spread to a large number of people across a large area, such as a country

evidence Anything, such as data or statistics, that proves or disproves something

factories Buildings where goods are made in large quantities

gender The state of being male or female

hybrids Vehicles that run on a combination of gasoline and electricity

industry Specific types of businesses that make or produce goods in factories to sell

interaction When two or more people spend time communicating with each other

Internet Service Provider (ISP) A company that provides its customers with access to the Internet and other Internet-related services, such as e-mail accounts

literacy The ability to read and write

logic A system of thinking and figuring out ideas

manufacturing plants The places where goods are made, by hand, by machines, or both

obesity A condition in which a person is very overweight

politicians People who are involved in politics, especially as officeholders

program To write a set of instructions for a computer or robot

qualified Having the qualities and knowledge for a job or function, usually as a result of education

repetitive Describes something that that is repeated many times

robots Machines that operate automatically with similar skills to humans

satellite A human-made object put in orbit around Earth to collect information or for communication

sensors Devices that detect such things as light, movement, or temperature, and send a message to a control center

social media Websites and other online locations or applications that people use to communicate or develop business or social contacts

software Computer programs that are used to operate a computer

source A person, organization, or publication from which information was obtained

statistics Facts involving numbers or data

taxes Money people pay to the government to finance services such as schools and hospitals

valid Something that is proven or well founded

versatile Able to adapt or be adapted to many different functions or activities

virtual reality (VR) An artificial environment created by computers

warehouses Buildings used for the storage of goods

wind drag Resistance caused by the wind

LEARNING MORE

Find out more about the arguments concerning modern technology.

Books

Amstutz, Lisa. *All About Robots* (Cutting-Edge Technology). Focus Readers, 2017.

Colby, Jennifer. *Data in Arguments* (21st Century Skills Library: Data Geek).
Cherry Lake Publishing, 2017.

Marsico, Katie. *Self-Driving Cars* (A True Book). Children's Press, 2016.

Swanson, Jennifer. *National Geographic Kids Everything Robotics.*
National Geographic Children's Books, 2016.

Websites

Learn all about writing arguments at:
www.icivics.org/products/drafting-board

Learn more about robotics on the National Aeronautics and Space Administration (NASA) website:
www.nasa.gov/audience/forstudents/5-8/features/nasa-knows/what_is_robotics_58.html

Find out what the United Nations Children's Fund (UNICEF) has to say about the issues around young people and technology:
www.unicefusa.org/stories/unicef-and-unicef-usa-call-empowering-children-digital-age/33748

Find out more about the history of the World Wide Web and its inventor's plans for its future:
https://webfoundation.org/about/vision/history-of-the-web

Learn how to write a good argument at:
https://writingcenter.unc.edu/tips-and-tools/argument

INDEX

ABOUT THE AUTHOR

Simon Rose is an author of 15 novels and more than 100 nonfiction books. He offers programs for schools, covering the writing process, editing and revision, where ideas come from, character development, historical fiction, story structure, and the publishing world. He is an instructor for adults and offers online workshops and courses. Simon also provides services for writers, including manuscript evaluation, editing, and coaching, plus copywriting services for the business community.